Bismillāhir-Rahmānir-Rahīm.
In The Name of God,
The Most Compassionate, The Most Merciful.

Gaze of Compassion

Sitti Rahman Bibi

Pearl Rain Publishing

About the cover: The heavenly olive tree, framed by 28 pearls signifying the 28 letters of the Arabic alphabet.

Gaze of Compassion
Copyright © 2021 by Sitti Rahman Bibi
ISBN 978-0-578-32502-6

All rights reserved. No part of this book may be reproduced or stored in a retrieval system or transmitted in any form by any means, electronic or mechanical, including copying, recording, or otherwise, without prior permission of the copyright owner.

Printed in the United States of America

Foreword

Sitti Rahman Bibi, in *The Gaze of Compassion*, is a "heavenly apprentice" who records the divine texts she receives with brave, luminous simplicity. The presences that she becomes aware of, around and within her, are apprehended through a practice of rapt, prayerful attention, receptive and searching. Given permission to guide and serve humanity in the traditional Sufi manner, she reminds us that we have the strength and courage to cleanse the doors of our perception and see things as they really are, and to walk out into the world as into our own hearts, receiving and offering the healing blessings of the "divine fruits of Allāh's Garden."

—Kythe Maryam Heller, ThD Candidate and Teaching Fellow, Harvard Divinity School

Heavenly Apprentice

There are small orange spheres in a geometric formation, connected by small metallic tubes. This formation exists on the earthly plane. It is aligned with and connected to the structure of the left side of the body of a true devotee. If a demon, such as an astral shark, sees the formation, it will consume the part of the spirit that accompanies the outline of the orange spheres. This outline may appear on one who is supposed to be in the heavens, but who uses an object that causes descension toward the earthly plane. As the elemental spirit meets the earth, the demonic shark smells the blood of that individual and consumes the outlined aspect of the elemental life. For example, if one takes a trip to the ocean and submerges in the deep waters, perhaps in the darkness of that sea area a shark may come along and consume the swimmer.

This exact thing happens when a devotee who has been awarded residence on the Green Square, which is the first heaven, and beyond plummets to the earth with an earthly device called a *mirror*, leaving him or herself as a victim to the sharks. This terrifying shark swims in the ocean of the night sky. The devotee might say, "Oh, I can look in the mirror and admire the youth and beauty that Allāh has blessed me with!" The devotee is aware of the sin of vanity, but is fearful of losing the gift of the beauty and youth in the face, and then allows his/her mind to convince them to check on what they were graced with. The mind says, "You must make sure to stop old age or the waning of your heavenly beauty. You have to stop your own mortality. So, check in the earthly mirror to resolve the possibility of approaching degradation." The mind offers clever and clear instructions in this way. If the devotee follows the mind's request, he or she will face destruction of the body, wisdom, and light.

    To stop the calamity of the persuasion of the mind, the devotee must ignore the mind's request, which holds tremendous *shakti,* and then refuse access to the earthly mirror for the sake of safety. When the devotee ignores the request from the mind and thereby avoids destruction, the devotee leaves the earthly form, transcending the seven colors in the ether, and dwells in Allāh's Kingdom. Their body will be on the earth, while their light-life dwells peacefully in Allāh's Kingdom, receiving commands from wise elders or great *qutbs* in the form of a map. These maps reveal the way in which the devotee can truly transform him or herself, as well as the way the devotee can truly help mankind in this time of destruction known as the *Kali Yuga*.

Anyone who wants to transcend will come to a point in which they cannot risk plummeting to earth from a high altitude, becoming victim to demonic life forms or forces. One who goes up must be careful. The devotee must enter Allāh's Garden, receive advice through instruction from Allāh's devotees, then dispel dark ignorance by applying what has been taught to him or her. The devotee will, through direct communication with heavenly dwellers, offer divine words as nourishment to seekers in the *dunyā*. The wisdom received by the devoted representative of Allāh, who is a heavenly apprentice, offers heavenly fruits in the form of words and text, freeing seekers from the inherent destruction of this *yuga*. The devotee gains maturity by severing the connection to the happiness and sorrow of the earthly body and then transcending to the heavens, dwelling without being captured by the clutches of arrogance and vanity. Dwellers of the *dunyā* will have the opportunity to seek guidance from a true heavenly being who has, in this *yuga* of destruction, graced the earth-world.

For clarity and guidance consult with Khidr ☺. Also, respond to the song of morning birds, who awaken all for prayer.

Khidr Nabī ﷺ and Majestic Lion

A heavenly angel, garbed in glistening white fabric and with beautiful wings, is seen under the Resplendence of The *Nūr*. With a scepter in hand, she acknowledges the presence of *olis* (lights of God). The *olis* affirm the direction of the Path of *Dīnul-Islām* (The Path Of Perfect Purity). The *olis* fly to a pink stone. As the *olis* meet the stone, a floral geometric pattern manifests on the surface of the stone. The inscription illuminates, while projecting a resonance that deciphers its symbolism. Then the inscription reappears on a path that forms below the pink stone. This path is composed of *navaratna*— the nine precious gems. The walkway of *navaratna,* which consists of gemstones that each repeat the pattern from the pink stone, leads to a palace guarded by a lion.

It is a large palace—a *masjid* beside a well. A dipper submerges itself into the well, then pours the water upon blank text. The book that has absorbed the well water transforms. Now the pages hold the light of nine precious gems: ruby, pearl, coral, hessonite, blue sapphire, cat's eye, yellow sapphire, emerald, and diamond. They proclaim Divine Wisdom. Then a date palm appears and offers its fruits.

The heavenly angel gathers dates and the text.

The angel hands the text and dates to one who meets the lion at the heavenly palace. This devotee is then offered a seat, with permission to share the many teachings of the jewel-adorned manuscript. The devotee may record several manuscripts from the single text received. The teachings may also be recited. The value of the book will call forth witnesses and guidance from the heavens.

While the devotee's light body is in the heavenly palace, his earthly body remains in the world, the *dunyā*, where a special guide appears and affirms the devotee as his apprentice. This guide is Khidr Nabī☺, the Green

Prophet, the Eternal Prophet, who walks among the dwellers of the earth-world to offer divine instruction. The apprentice who acquires discipleship must seek clarity and guidance from Khidr☺, while obtaining access to an eternal water source The divine spring pours forth generously as it quenches thirst, and it offers medicinal healing remedies and Divine Wisdom while restoring the apprentice's youthful appearance. One who studies under Khidr☺, obediently following instructions, gains the wealth of this mysterious water supply.

Khidr Nabī ☺ appears to guide when called upon. As the apprentice asks a question, Khidr☺ answers, using anything in existence from any of the

18,000 universes. To answer a question, he will instantly summon the person, plant-life, place, or object that must reveal the answer. The object physically appears before the apprentice and reveals the answer with its *own* language. For example, if a question is asked and an herb appears, the healing properties of the herb will speak of its benefits to the apprentice. As the herb speaks of its value, the devotee acquires the benefit of the herb's medicinal properties. Therefore, the apprentice may not necessarily need to buy the herb, because healing was obtained through direct transmission. Another way the guidance of Khidr☺ is provided is through warning. (The heavenly angels also warn.) Khidr☺

may warn of the impending threat of *shaitan*. In this case, *shaitan* may take form surrounded by fire. The fire may represent the destructive outcome of his presence. If this occurs, the apprentice must pray, helping to dispel the darkness that accompanies satanic force. Later, the apprentice may even be able to walk into the calamity that has been resolved through divine intervention. The apprentice will become witness to the dissipation of harm, which, without his/her prayer, might have resulted in destruction.

To continue to receive instruction from Khidr Nabī ☺, the apprentice must maintain proximity. Ignorant actions and bad qualities can create a distance or obstacle, preventing access to Khidr ☉. If this happens, the apprentice must reflect, correcting him/herself to regain proximity. A true disciple will value the guidance of Khidr Nabī ☉ and make the intention to not stray from *Dīnul-Islām,* The Path Of Perfect Purity. Because the apprentice ingests water of *Ākhirah,* exploration beyond becomes accessible, or permissible. The devotee can sit or lie down, while their light-life within journeys to heavenly spheres.

    Meanwhile, at the prayer palace guarded by the majestic lion, another type of study is initiated: apprenticeship before the heavenly lion—The Lion of Allāh, ʿAlī ☉. As ʿAlī takes his position by the well beside the palace, heavenly maidens join. Pages of jeweled texts emerge from the well, as dates and other produce from Allāh's Garden are distributed among heavenly dwellers. As the teachings of the well's text resonate through the atmosphere, the devotee also has earthly residence in the *dunyā* and records the text, through writing and words, to offer seekers in the earth-world. Many seekers in the *dunyā* can then correct themselves, having received divine teachings from a divine source.

For clarity and guidance consult with Khidr ☉. Also, respond to the song of morning birds, who awaken all for prayer.

Tasbīh and
The Lamp

Tasbīh beads with a beautiful beaded tassle glisten luminously under the Resplendence of the *Nūr.* An *oli* affirms the grace that the beads hold. There are more olis appearing to affirm the value of these beads. These heavenly beads are offered to one who surrenders to Allāh, giving up the attraction and connection to the *dunyā.* The *dunyā* within the heart flies away as the light-life within resplends, while the *tasbīh* beads settle in hand. The devotee will drink the water of the heart's well and receive the fruits of the *Sidratul-Muntahā*.

The devotee's Sheikh will appear, advising him/her to overcome the connection to sleep and to pray through the night as if it were daytime. Heavenly saints and wise elders will be able to offer seekers of truth wise council through the devotee. For this reason, the devotee will have the protection of the lion by the well. The devotee must drink from the well to remain under the lion's protection.

As the devotee records divine text on paper, a radiance of peace from the heavenly olive fills the atmosphere. Then the olive releases its oil into a subtle lamp that is beside the devotee. As seekers of truth approach, the devotee will open his/her hand and gaze at the palm. The reflected image of the people in hand will receive the healing olive oil through the gaze of the devotee. The seekers will keep walking past the devotee, subtly receiving the medicinal healing agent of the heavenly olive. The devotee looks in hand and sees the seekers as they walk by. They are not aware of the administered ointment or of the protection of the devotee that is provided by the lion, enforced by the Command of Allāh. Because of the seekers' connection to the earth, they may not be able to perceive the miraculous essence of the olive tree that has originated in Allāh's Garden.

    Allāh's magnificent garden produces fruits, herbs, plants, vegetation, and grasses that can heal others if accessed. A devotee who has access can reap Allāh's harvest from Allāh's Garden and offer it to mankind through his/her gaze. The devotee will gaze in hand while the oils and essences of exalted plant-life improve the thought processes of others, as well as deter dangers that may approach the seekers. The power of the gaze is given to a devotee who has a seat by the well. *Alhamdulillāh.*

One who is awarded a seat can teach and help others. He/she will inspire others to follow the Straight Path and overcome the destruction that is caused by evil actions, bad words, bad thoughts, as well as sins.

Fragrance wafts forth from the devotee, calling on people who want to be free. The seekers will walk toward the devotee, even though they may be worlds apart. The devotee will gaze in hand, as they step in the direction of Light. *Āmīn.*

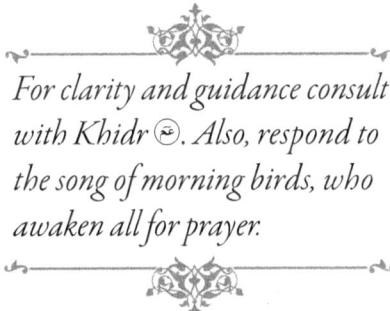

For clarity and guidance consult with Khidr ☺. Also, respond to the song of morning birds, who awaken all for prayer.

Glossary

Alhamdulillāh (Arabic) All praise is to God.

Dīnul-Islām (Arabic) The Way Of *Islām*. The Path Of Perfect Purity, along which one proceeds with absolute certainty, surrender, and faith in Allah.

Dunyā (Arabic) The world of material and physical forms, which consists of configurations of the five elements. All things in the material world are subject to change and have a finite span of existence.

Masjid (Arabic) Mosque. Lit. a place of prostration.

Navaratna (Sanskrit) Nine Gems. Esoterically, the *Navaratna* correlate and interrelate with the openings in the human body, celestial bodies in the solar system, and properties of Divine Wisdom.

Oli (Tamil) Light. Oli may refer to a being who is a "light of God". Interestingly, *oli* is also a Latin derivative, whose meaning is "olive".

Qutb (Arabic) This word translates as "axis" or "pole". Spiritually, it signifies an indispensable central axis around which all of the cosmos revolve. In Sufism, a *qutb* is an emanation of God's Light, manifesting as a Perfect Human Being who awakens and illuminates humanity with explanations of Divine Wisdom and Truth.

Shakti (Sanskrit) Primordial cosmic energy arising from the five elements, generating the dynamic powers of creation and all manifestations subject to temporal change.

Sidratul-Muntahā (Arabic) The Divine Lote Tree Of The Farthest Boundary, demarcating the utmost border of the seventh heaven, beyond which none can pass, among both angels and humankind. The sole exception is the Prophet Muhammad ﷺ who, bodily, surpassed its limit and attained direct presence before the Throne of Allāh. Within this divine communion, the instruction for *salāt* (the five-times prayer) was revealed to him.

shaitan (Arabic) satan. The embodiment of the inclination to do evil. *Shaitan* is a fire-entity, born of the fires of arrogance, pride, anger, jealousy, and other egotistically destructive qualities and actions.

Tasbīh (Arabic) Prayer beads. *Tasbīh* signifies "to glorify something". The affirmation *Subhān-Allāh*— Glory be to God— derives from the same Arabic verbal root. A Muslim tasbīh will generally have 33 or 99 beads, signifying the *Asmā'ul-Husnā,* The Ninety-Nine Beautiful Names Of Allāh.

Yuga (Sanskrit) An epoch, a cosmic cycle of existence. There are several *yugas,* each one existing for a period of millions of years. The universe is currently traversing the *Kali Yuga,* an era of materialism, illusion, and ignorance. Despite the obstacles, it is always up to each individual to unveil and venerate the undiminishing Inner Light.

About the Author

Sitti Rahman Bibi grew up under the loving guidance of a Sufi Saint, Muhammad Raheem Bawa Muhaiyaddeen, may Allāh be pleased with him. Throughout her childhood, she spent hours listening to and absorbing his compassionate wisdom, observing his exemplary conduct. Since his passing from this world, his living teachings have sustained her as she visits and explores subtle realms, acquiring insights into the vast wonders and mysteries of God's Creation. Her path is a unique and demanding one, calling upon her to be ever-present, attentive, disciplined, and dutiful. It is her hope that, in sharing her direct experiences and understandings, she may help others to find clarity, comfort, and peace amidst a world of turmoil and confusion.

Inshā'allāh, this is the first of a series of small books by Sitti Rahman Bibi. They manifest through an interesting process of transmission. Sitti Rahman faithfully documents her visions in accord with specific guided instructions, frequently writing during the hours before the dawn. Because she is physically unable to re-write them outside the domain of revelation, she later relates the words to the editor to again transcribe. Finally, having lightly edited the narrative, they read through it together for clearness and accuracy.

May these revelations open the way to a shared journey into divine realization and inspiration. May they turn yearning hearts toward the Gracious Qualities of Allāh's Eternal Kingdom.

Other Books by Sitti Rahman Bibi

Wooden Hand, Luminous Hand
TREASURES OF AN EXALTED JOURNEY

This book reveals mystical treasures along a path explored through prayerful meditation. A map in the Hand illumines a journey of discovery leading to divine nourishment, reflection, and wisdom.

*If you want to see yourself,
It will show your reflection.
If you want to quench your thirst,
Or cleanse yourself,
It will show where to find water.*

*To end hunger
Fruits of wisdom will appear.
If you want to become small and hidden,
You will see a hiding place.
If you want to see the prayer state
of the true believers,
They will come.*

ISBN 979-8-218-62215-2
8.5 x 11 inches / Paperback / 132 pages / $25.00 from Amazon.com

(Continued on next page)

Other Books by Sitti Rahman Bibi, cont'd

Pearl Flame
SECOND EDITION

Guidance received from revelation and the importance of that revelation in this time. Through meditation we may access Inner Scripture and, in turn, share that scripture to guide and benefit others.

"One must search within and find that house of worship. Those who are born as human beings must receive the revelations that will fall like rain at this time. Their revelations will change those who have been led astray and guide them to the Ocean of *Ilm* (divine knowledge), where the light boat will save them. The birds of the hereafter will awaken them for prayer. There, people will be forever nourished by Allāh's food of grace."

ISBN 979-8-218-62205-3
8.5 x 11 inches / Paperback / 96 pages / $15.00 from Amazon.com

www.ingramcontent.com/pod-product-compliance
Lightning Source LLC
Chambersburg PA
CBHW061518040426
42450CB00008B/1682